MW00528285

PAST & PRESENT

NEWBERG

OPPOSITE: The south side of Newberg has historically been a residential area, and that is still the case today. The neighborhood has filled out nicely; in addition to many more homes, there are now multiple churches, schools, and parks in this section of town. (Courtesy Yamhill County Historical Society.)

PAST & PRESENT

NEWBERG

Britta Mansfield

To all who do not yet know they love history. May this book pique your interest and encourage you to learn more.

Copyright © 2023 by Britta Mansfield
ISBN 978-1-4671-6067-4

Library of Congress Control Number: 2023941789

Published by Arcadia Publishing
Charleston, South Carolina

Printed in the United States of America

For all general information, please contact Arcadia Publishing:
Telephone 843-853-2070
Fax 843-853-0044
E-mail sales@arcadiapublishing.com

Visit us on the Internet at www.arcadiapublishing.com

ON THE FRONT COVER: Looking west down First Street in the 1930s reveals much of Newberg's downtown core. Traffic flowed in both directions, and businesses lined the streets. First Street in 2023 has not changed much. Active businesses still sit on either side of the street, but today, traffic only flows in one direction. (Past image, courtesy Oregon Historical Society; present image, author's collection.)

ON THE BACK COVER: Chehalem Valley Mills is no longer operational, but the vacant building can still be seen along Main Street. (Courtesy George Fox University.)

Contents

ACKNOWLEDGMENTS

First, I must give thanks to God for giving me the skills and passion to complete this project.

This book is not a product of just my own work. Many others have been preserving, researching, interpreting, and teaching, and their work made this book possible. Caitlin Corning and Rachel Thomas led an incredible team of students who completed the George Fox University Mapping Our History project. They researched most of the buildings in downtown Newberg and made their findings easily and publicly accessible. Their work was a huge benefit for this book and simplified my research process.

The Newberg Area Historical Society laid the groundwork for this work with its downtown signage project. Its members also presented lectures that contributed to my understanding of the city.

The George Fox University Archives were immensely helpful. The team of Dustin Kelley, Jessica Truesdell, and student employee Henry Clancy helped gather and scan many of the photographs in this book. Jessica was especially helpful and accommodated an outlandish number of last-minute requests.

My amazing husband, Matthew, was my biggest supporter through this whole process. Thank you for pushing me to finish this; being the best father to Christine, especially while I was working; and going on numerous walks with me to photograph old buildings. My parents were wonderful through this process, and were champion babysitters. Christine has also been a joy and a wonderful baby to have during this time. She provided many happy breaks as I researched, wrote, photographed, and edited.

Lastly, I would like to thank the repositories who are preserving the historic photographs seen in this book. All historic images were collected from the George Fox University Archives (GFU), the Oregon Historical Society (OHS), or the Yamhill County Historical Society (YCHS). All present images were taken by the author.

INTRODUCTION

Newberg, Oregon, is a relatively small community of about 25,000 people roughly 40 minutes outside of Portland in the Willamette Valley. It has been occupied for centuries, beginning with the Kalapuya people who are today members of the Confederated Tribes of the Grand Ronde. Some of the earliest white settlers came in the 1830s and 1840s and included Ewing Young and Joseph Rogers. Both of them impacted the region that became Newberg, but neither established lasting settlements here.

By the 1880s, many members of the Friends church, often referred to as Quakers, began journeying to Newberg to build a new community. William Hobson was a Quaker leader who visited in 1876. He was impressed by the natural beauty and opportunity he saw in the Chehalem Valley and encouraged his contemporaries to move west.

Jesse Edwards came to Newberg in 1881 as an answer to Hobson's call. He purchased nearly 184 acres of land, had it surveyed and platted, and gave Newberg much of the structure it builds upon today. His first home in Newberg was sold to John and Laura Minthorn, who invited their orphaned nephew Herbert Hoover to come live with them. Hoover eventually became the 31st president of the United States, but long before that he was one of the first students at Friends Pacific Academy. The academy was established by the early Quaker community in Newberg and eventually grew into what is now George Fox University, a top Christian college in Oregon.

Agriculture has been an essential part of life in Newberg. Berries and hazelnuts were common early crops, and many of the first industrial buildings were used to process them. Starting in the mid- to late 20th century, the agricultural focus shifted to grapes and wine making. Some of the Willamette Valley's first wine grapes were planted in and around Newberg.

Community has remained an important element of life in Newberg even through all the change and growth. There seems to be a little something for everyone in this corner of Yamhill County. As the modern photographs in this book eventually become historic in their own right, hopefully they will showcase how Newberg has remained a great place to grow.

CHAPTER 1

CHURCHES

Welcome to Newberg! Most of the town's entrances are marked with welcome signs. The signs have been updated through the years, but used to stand on each side of the road as one entered town. (Courtesy OHS.)

Newberg was founded primarily by Quakers who migrated westward in the 1880s and 1890s. William Hobson was one of the first to make the journey. He was followed by Jesse Edwards and hundreds of others eager to start a new community in Oregon. This historic Quaker church was built in 1891, and weekly services are still held there today. It sits on the original site of Friends Pacific Academy, which later became George Fox University. The school was moved across town to its current location, and the church was built in its place. (Past image, courtesy GFU.)

There are multiple Friends churches in Newberg today. One of them is the North Valley Friends Church, which was established in 1972 after Chehalem Center Friends and Springbrook Friends combined. The community around the church has grown, and the property is now bordered by a school and neighborhood. (Past image, courtesy GFU.)

Many churches in Newberg meet in historic buildings. One such church is La Iglesia Evangelica Los Amigo, which meets in this historic building on the corner of Second and College Streets. The space was initially constructed for First Christian Church and is now occupied by a Spanish-speaking congregation. (Past image, courtesy GFU.)

In the 1920s, this Nazarene church neighbored First Christian Church on Second Street. Both buildings featured impressive stairways at their entrances. The Nazarene church is no longer standing, and an apartment complex has been built on its site. (Past image, courtesy GFU.)

Many of Newberg's early settlers practiced their Christian faith in the Friends or Quaker tradition. However, other denominations were also present in the town. This Presbyterian church sat next to the Carnegie Library and was across the street from a Methodist church. Today, the space is occupied by First American Title Insurance Company. (Past image, courtesy GFU.)

PRESBYTERIAN CHURCH, NEWBERG, OREGON.   W-22.

Some of the Willamette Valley's earliest Catholics settled in St. Paul, on the opposite side of the river from Newberg. However, there were a number of Catholic townspeople in Newberg during its early days. By 1908, St. Peter's Catholic Church was built on Main Street. St. Peter's has gathered in two other Newberg buildings, and its original space is now home to the Calvary Chapel congregation. (Past image, courtesy GFU.)

5250　METHODIST CHURCH, NEWBERG, ORE.

There were multiple Methodist churches throughout Newberg. One was on the southeast corner of Hancock and Howard Streets, and another was on the northeast corner of Third and Grant Streets. Red Hills Church still meets in the Grant Street location, while the corner of Hancock and Howard Streets is now occupied by a real estate office. (Past image, courtesy YCHS.)

CHURCHES

Newberg's first
Baptist church
initially met
at the corner
of College and
Sheridan Streets.
The building was
updated multiple
times at this
location before
moving out of the
downtown. A lovely
residence now sits
on the site of the
original church.
(Past image,
courtesy GFU.)

There are two Baptist churches in Newberg today. Grace Baptist grew out of the original congregation that met at College and Sheridan Streets. Its building was recently updated to better accommodate the needs of the congregation and community. (Past image, courtesy GFU.)

SCHOOLS

A set of Newberg gates welcomes both residents and visitors to town. The gates have been replaced with colorful signs that feature iconic Newberg items like grapes and camellias. (Courtesy GFU.)

Schools have been present in Newberg as long as children have been present. One of the earliest public schools was a one-room schoolhouse on the corner of Illinois and Main Streets built in 1881. Residential buildings have since been constructed on its original site, and Newberg has added many schools to keep up with its growing population. (Past image, courtesy GFU.)

Named after trapper and early Newberg resident Ewing Young, this school sits a few miles outside of town. It was not part of the Newberg School District until 1962. The original building has been replaced, but an active elementary school still stands in its place. (Past image, courtesy GFU.)

One of Newberg's most memorable schools was Central School. The site served as a school from 1905 to 1995. Just like many of Newberg's historic buildings, this one underwent renovations to accommodate its growing student body. After educational operations ceased in the building, its interior was remodeled so the space could become a cultural center. Now known as the Chehalem Cultural Center, it remains an integral part of the Newberg community. (Past image, courtesy OHS.)

CENTRAL SCHOOL-NEWBERG.ORE.

More schools were quickly needed as Newberg's population grew. The Harding School was built in 1923. It has housed a public school, a Catholic school, and C.S. Lewis Academy. The building has recently been converted into an upscale apartment community. (Past image, courtesy OHS.)

No. 17. HIGH SCHOOL, NEWBERG ORE.

This building was constructed in 1911 as the first high school. It was eventually used as a middle school and today holds Newberg School District offices. Edwards Elementary School shares the property and sits just behind this building. The district is working on a construction project adjacent to this building to better serve its students. (Past image, courtesy GFU.)

Many may recognize Springbrook as the name of a road, shopping center, or various housing developments in Newberg. However, Springbrook used to be a separate community; it even had its own school. The school was expanded multiple times and eventually became part of the Newberg School District. The old building now sits vacant and can be seen when driving through the area. (Past image, courtesy YCHS.)

George Fox University has been a constant educational institution in Newberg since its founding. The school was known as Friends Pacific Academy when it opened, and the future president Herbert Hoover was one of its first pupils. Minthorn Hall was one of the original structures and now sits on the main quad of campus, still used for classes and offices. (Past image, courtesy GFU.)

Another original George Fox building came to be called Hoover Hall. This building and Minthorn Hall were originally constructed where the Newberg Friends Church stands today. They were both moved to the current campus location as the school grew and just before the church was built. The original Hoover building is no longer standing, but a new structure has been constructed and is also named after President Hoover. (Past image, courtesy GFU.)

Quaker College Campus - Newberg Oregon

christia
5-100S

As the college grew, additional buildings were needed. Two volunteers, Amanda Woodward and Evangeline Martin, raised nearly $30,000 for the construction of Wood-Mar Hall. The building had space for classes and an auditorium. In 1994, the Edwards-Holman Science Center was built and connected to Wood-Mar Hall to stabilize the historic structure. Both buildings are used today and are instantly recognizable campus features. (Past image, courtesy GFU.)

SCHOOLS

Ezra Woodward was one of the founders of Friends Pacific Academy, the school that became George Fox University. His home sits on the corner of River and Hancock Streets and was built before the school was moved to its current location. It is no longer a residence but serves as the campus health and counseling center. (Past image, courtesy GFU.)

George Hartley was one of the early professors at Friends Pacific Academy. His house was across a canyon made by Hess Creek, which runs through campus, and a bridge was built to reach the Hartley home. The original bridge does not remain, but two others now stretch across the canyon, and students use them daily. (Past image, courtesy GFU.)

SCHOOLS

Levi Pennington served as the president of George Fox University from 1911 to 1941. This building, which now houses the George Fox University Honors Program, was originally his home. During his nearly 30 years as president, Pennington led the college through many changes. Some were small changes to campus and how the school operated, and some were responses to major world events like World War I. (Past image, courtesy GFU.)

Weesner House is named after Oliver Weesner, a professor at the college during the first half of the 20th century. The building was completed in 1924 and renovated in 1980. The house serves as on-campus housing today, along with various dormitories and apartment buildings. (Past image, courtesy GFU.)

In addition to Pennington House, Pennington Hall was also named after Levi Pennington. This residence hall was built in 1962 and accommodates 112 students. Most recently renovated in 2014, it is conveniently located on the main quad of campus near a number of academic buildings. (Past image, courtesy GFU.)

Weesner Village was named after Oliver Weesner. These apartments were built in 1962 and originally designated for married students. As the student body grew, single students also lived in them. The whole complex can now hold 36 students, with three living in each apartment. (Past image, courtesy GFU.)

George Fox students have had a long-standing interest in sports. The first dedicated gymnasium was built in 1910 by combining two barns. Today, students have multiple options for engaging in various athletic programming. The Hadlock Student Center is where students can enjoy various forms of recreation such as rock climbing and weight lifting. The building also features an indoor track, volleyball and basketball courts, and yoga and dance studios. (Past image, courtesy GFU.)

Construction on Hester Gymnasium began in 1945. The building replaced the original gym and enabled students to continue enjoying athletic programs at the college. By 1977, a larger facility was needed, so Wheeler Sports Center was built. George Fox University basketball and volleyball games are played here every season. (Past image, courtesy GFU.)

The university purchased this former military building in 1948. It initially served as the dining hall and later became the fine arts building. The current dining hall sits across campus and has space for student and community events as well as daily meals. (Past image, courtesy GFU.)

The Klages building was completed in 1958 and originally served as a dining hall and student union building. It is central to campus and has housed various dining and recreation options through the years. The building is currently used for the Maker Hub, a collaborative design space used largely by engineering students, and the campus bookstore. (Past image, courtesy GFU.)

A library is a central feature of any university. Gilbert and Olive Shambaugh must have thought so because they donated $275,000 for the construction of Shambaugh Library in 1960. The structure served the college well and featured an outdoor fountain. The Murdock Library replaced Shambaugh in 1988 and continues to provide students with ample resources for research and study. (Past image, courtesy GFU.)

Brougher Hall was built in 1947 and was originally used for science classes and labs. At one point, it even housed the college museum, which featured an extensive collection. Today, it sits on the main quad of campus, adjacent to a rose garden, and is currently used by art students. (Past image, courtesy GFU.)

SCHOOLS

The Lemmons Center, completed in 1965, is one of the most architecturally interesting buildings on campus. It was designed to look like a water molecule with three hexagonal sections. Classrooms are located along the outside of the building, and a large lecture hall sits in the middle. It continues to be used by students and has been home to various fields of study through the years. (Past image, courtesy GFU.)

Since Hess Creek Canyon runs through campus, multiple bridges cross it to help everyone get from place to place. This bridge connects students from a residence hall and parking lot to the Wheeler Sports Center. (Past image, courtesy GFU.)

3

BUSINESSES

Newberg gates are seen here as a car departs the center of town. Travel between towns has always been important, whether on foot, on the river, on horses, in trains, or in cars. (Courtesy OHS.)

OLD RAMSEY MILL AND DAM.
NEWBERG. OREGON.

Wood mills, gristmills, flour mills, pulp mills, and paper mills were necessary as people began settling in Newberg. They provided employment and resources. The David Ramsey Mill was one of the earliest in town and was operational until 1862. (Past image, courtesy YCHS.)

BUSINESSES

The Spaulding Mill was an integral establishment for much of Newberg's history. Even through multiple operators, the site employed hundreds over the years. A mill was active on this site until 2015 but has since been demolished with plans for redevelopment. (Past image, courtesy OHS.)

The paper mill seemed to be a constant feature of Newberg until it closed in 2015. The mill at this site was initially opened by the Spaulding family but passed through many owners after the Spauldings sold it. Its closure in 2015 marked a time of intense transition for those who had worked there and for the surrounding community. (Past image, courtesy OHS.)

PULP MILL, NEWBERG, OREGON.

Chehalem Valley Mills sat on Main Street, where most of Newberg's early business district developed. The mill processed grains and flour directly across the street from the Hotel Purdy. Many of the mill buildings remain today; however, they are vacant and not operational. (Past image, courtesy GFU.)

The Springbrook Cannery was the economic center of the small community. It was established in 1903 but did not begin operating until 1904. Berries, cherries, peaches, and prunes were some of the common crops of the region, and canning became a convenient way to preserve them. Canned products were sold locally and sent to other places, like Portland. (Past image, courtesy YCHS.)

The Springbrook Cannery was opened by a co-operative called the Springbrook Canning and Preserving Company. The cannery expanded through the years and eventually processed more than just fruit, canning various vegetables and offering some of its products frozen. Crops from beyond the Newberg area were brought in for processing. The cannery operated under multiple names and owners; when it closed in 1969, it was owned by Flav-R-Pac. (Past image, courtesy YCHS.)

The Newberg Packing Company is mentioned as early as 1891 and was on the corner of First and College Streets from at least 1907. The Francis Theater stood on the site after meatpacking operations ceased. The facility processed meat from Newberg and as far away as Portland. The site is now known as Francis Square and is a small park in the middle of downtown. (Past image, courtesy OHS.)

Just as in neighboring Springbrook, berries were the prominent crop for years in Newberg. There were many fruit dryers, processing plants, and even a juice plant in town that all helped manage the region's delicious fruits. One of the town's many processing facilities was the Allen Fruit Company. It became what is today PPM Technologies, which designs and builds food production and processing equipment. (Past image, courtesy GFU.)

Much of Newberg and the surrounding area was settled as agricultural land. Other industries were necessary though, and so among the fruit dryers, mills, and retail shops there was also a tile factory. It sat right next to the train tracks on the north side of town. Today, a Habitat For Humanity ReStore sits near where the factory used to operate. (Past image, courtesy GFU.)

Today, Newberg residents looking to buy a home or piece of property can connect with a number of real estate offices in town. Years ago, people would have gone to the Newberg Land Company. A blacksmith shop had been at this location before the land company opened, and after it closed, shoe stores, barbers, apparel shops, and accountants have all occupied the space. Today, it is home to Taqueria El Burrito, a Mexican restaurant. (Past image, courtesy GFU.)

Transportation was essential even before cars were available. Horses and carriages were one of the primary modes of travel. They required quite a bit of care and needed their own shelter. Livery stables provided some of that care and shelter. The site on the corner of First and School Streets was a livery before becoming an auto garage. A local law office, Brown, Tarlow, Bridges & Palmer, operates on the site today. (Past image, courtesy YCHS.)

Trains soon came to Newberg, offering people another form of transportation. When the Red Electric ran down First Street, its ticket office sat where El Gordito Feliz is today. Sanborn fire insurance maps show that it had a lobby and waiting area as well as a baggage room. The building adjacent to it was a movie theater. Other businesses including an auto shop, coffee shop, and even a bakery operated out of the site at various times. (Past image, courtesy OHS.)

As soon as motor vehicles became widely available, auto shops and garages were abundant in Newberg. One of them sat at 113 Main Street. The site of the long since demolished garage is now occupied by a convenience store. (Past image, courtesy OHS.)

A 1929 Sanborn map shows six auto shops or garages along First Street. Not all remaining pictures are clearly identified, but at one point there was an auto shop roughly where Nap's Thriftway sits today. The grocery story was originally opened across the street but has been at its current location since 1946. (Past image, courtesy GFU.)

Main Street was once the center for business and industry in Newberg. Train tracks intersect the road, which made it easy for nearby fruit dryers and mills to load and unload products. Its proximity to the railroad tracks also made Main Street an ideal location for a hotel. The Hotel Purdy sat where Nara Teriyaki is today and was a convenient stop for those coming to Newberg. (Past image, courtesy GFU.)

The Union Block building is recognizable to most who live in Newberg. It sits on the corner of College and First Streets and has housed many popular businesses through the years. It has been occupied by banks, lawyers, retail shops, and even a hotel. An eye doctor's office, Coldwell Banker, and a local coffee shop can be found in the space today as well as apartments on the second story. (Past image, courtesy OHS.)

Morris, Miles & Co was the first occupant of what is now the oldest commercial building in Newberg that is still operational. The building has been used as a hardware store for most of its life. During the 1970s and 1980s, there was a discount store and a fitness center. The current occupant, Chapters Books and Coffee, opened in the early 2000s. The building has been renovated quite a bit since it was constructed but recently underwent facade work to restore the historic nature of the entrance. (Past image, courtesy GFU.)

Hardware stores are another necessity for a burgeoning town. Newberg has had many through the years. One of them was at 206 East First Street. By the 1940s, the business expanded and began selling furniture. Johnson's Furniture still operates in the same space today. (Past image, courtesy OHS.)

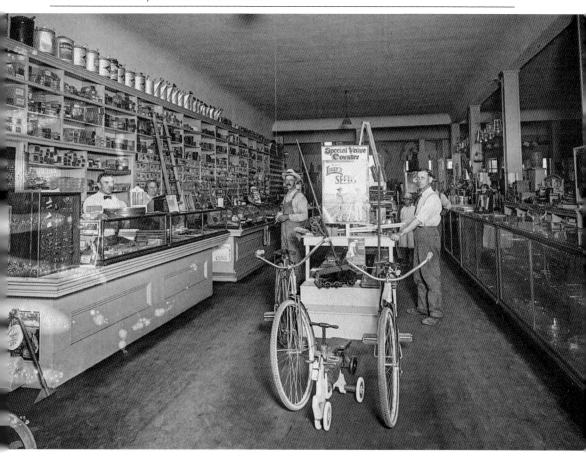

One of Newberg's first banks was on the corner of First and Meridian Streets in a building that also housed the *Newberg Graphic* newspaper offices. The bank closed long ago, and the *Graphic* now has an office just up the road. The brick facade of the building has been covered, but multiple businesses still use the space today. The second story also features cozy apartment spaces. (Past image, courtesy GFU.)

Many of Newberg's downtown buildings have seen a significant amount of turnover. However, the corner of First and Washington Streets was a bank from the late 1800s to the early 2000s. After the bank left, Cliff Creek Cellars opened a wine tasting room in the first-floor portion of the building. (Past image, courtesy GFU.)

Another one of downtown Newberg's buildings that has been used by multiple businesses is the space currently occupied by Hopp Insurance. In the early 1900s, it was Moore's Pharmacy, and through the last century, it has been used by a dairy, a meat market, and a home supply store. (Past image, courtesy GFU.)

Many businesses have occupied this building, with one of the earliest being a tinner and plumber. Others have included an auto parts store, athletic business, and a law firm. HBH Consulting Engineers currently occupy the front portion of the building, with a hair salon and alterations businesses in spaces along Howard Street. There are multiple housing units above the businesses. (Past image, courtesy GFU.)

From restaurants to retail space, this building has seen many different industries. Hardware stores, a furniture store, a music store, an appliance dealer, and Bowman's Restaurant have all occupied the building on the corner of First and Blaine Streets. Today, one can visit it as Lucky Fortune, a Chinese restaurant. (Past image, courtesy GFU.)

This corner lot borders the property where Herbert Hoover lived as a child. It was a service station for years and is seen here as a Plaid Pantry. Today, it is still a convenience store known as Mini Market El Tala. (Past image, courtesy GFU.)

The Union Block building has several individual retail spaces. Miller Mercantile and Coast to Coast were two of the longest occupants of this particular unit. Coldwell Banker currently has a large office in the location. Its opening marks a shift away from retail to a more business and administrative use for this unit. (Past image, courtesy GFU.)

The corner of First and Howard Streets has one of the more varied histories of the downtown buildings. The space was originally a church and then became an undertaker and furniture business. It eventually became a real estate office and then an office supply store known as Dent's. In the 2000s, it was sold multiple times. It is currently operated by Social Goods, a family-friendly gathering space serving local beer, wine, and food. (Past image, courtesy GFU.)

The inside of Social Goods still has some of the same features seen in Dent's. Although there is now a bar, and refrigerators line the walls, the impressive chandelier is still displayed from the ceiling, and the second-story balcony is open for restaurant seating. (Past image, courtesy GFU.)

Ice cream shops add a bit of flavor to any downtown. Dairy Queen sits on the west end of Newberg's downtown and provides tasty treats to the whole city. The structure has been rebuilt multiple times, most recently after a fire in 2015. A vintage Dairy Queen sign remains on the site and is a fun reminder that ice cream has been enjoyed by generations of people in Newberg. (Past image, courtesy GFU.)

Newberg's current city hall building was completed in 1913. Before that, a wooden structure on the same site housed both city hall and the fire department. The new building housed city hall as well as the police and fire departments. A fire caused serious damage in the 1990s, but the building was eventually restored and is occupied today by just city hall. (Past image, courtesy GFU.)

The first library in Newberg was operated out of a YMCA building on First Street just east of the current location. The library quickly needed more space. The Newberg Carnegie Library opened in 1912. Residents loved the new building so much that when more space was needed, they decided to expand the structure rather than look for a new space. The expanded library has been operational since 1986. (Past image, courtesy GFU.)

Newberg was named by Sebastian Brutscher, the first postmaster, who named it after his hometown in Bavaria. He ran the post office from his home, and as the town grew, a much larger establishment was needed. The current post office was built in 1936 and sits on First Street, central to the downtown businesses. (Past image, courtesy OHS.)

4

AROUND TOWN

Today, the signs at the entrances to Newberg all have the phrase "A Great Place to Grow," and that is certainly something the town has done and continues to do. The following images showcase some of that growth around town. (Courtesy OHS.)

FIRST STREET, NEWBERG, OREGON.

First Street can be seen here in the 1930s. Both large buildings on the left and right remain and are occupied by active businesses. The biggest difference between the two photographs is that First Street is now a one-way street and connected to Oregon's 99W Highway. (Past image, courtesy OHS.)

Trains were not only used to transport goods; they also made it easier for people to get from one place to another. The Red Electric train was operated by Southern Pacific and allowed people to easily travel between Portland and Newberg. The train ran along much of First Street, and when it was decommissioned, the tracks running down the street were paved over. (Past image, courtesy OHS.)

Not much remains from this historic image of First Street. Businesses remain in many of these locations, but the buildings themselves have been heavily updated or rebuilt completely. The historic image was taken facing east; looking closely, the old city hall and fire station can barely be made out on the left. (Past image, courtesy GFU.)

AROUND TOWN

First Street, looking East, Newberg, Oregon

As Newberg has grown and changed, so has its downtown. Businesses have shifted from essential services like grocery and hardware stores to retail spaces, restaurants, and wine tasting rooms. The First National Bank building is seen here on the right. The space now operates as DAnu Tasting Room. (Past image, courtesy GFU.)

Around Town

When driving to Newberg from Portland on Highway 99W, the first part of town travelers see is what used to be the separate community of Springbrook. Now officially part of Newberg, Springbrook has changed quite a bit. The cannery that was central to the community no longer stands. New developments have been built all around, and residential space surrounds what used to be the economic center of a small community. (Past image, courtesy YCHS.)

These unidentified buildings stood at the intersection of First and Main Streets where two highways—99W and 240—connect. The building on the northwest corner, constructed in 2023, is currently occupied by an accountant. (Past image, courtesy GFU.)

Today, Newberg celebrates the Old Fashioned Festival every year in July. Before the Old Fashioned Festival was established, residents participated in the Berrian Festival and later Farmeroo, which is pictured here. A parade is still held every year, although it no longer travels down First Street. The buildings in the background are still standing today, but they have not been used by parade watchers in quite a few years. (Past image, courtesy YCHS.)

AROUND TOWN

Meridian Street, Newberg, Ore.

E. C. KROPP CO. PUB. MILWAUKEE, NO. 1265

Newberg's neighborhoods have grown just as much as its downtown. Meridian Street still frames George Fox University and now runs through a lovely neighborhood full of both historic and modern homes. (Past image, courtesy GFU.)

The Edward's Home 402 So, College, before being moved.

Jesse Edwards was responsible for much of Newberg's settlement starting in the 1880s. He purchased a large portion of land on the south side of town and began selling pieces to those who wished to live there. He built and briefly lived in the Hoover-Minthorn House and then moved a few blocks west to this house, which is still a residential home, across from Newberg Friends Church. (Past image, courtesy GFU.)

AROUND TOWN

Here, the Royal Rosarians are pictured during the 1925 Berrian Festival; some of the houses seen behind the Rosarians are still standing today. The Newberg Old Fashioned Festival is still held every year at Memorial Park. The park is a wonderful year-round resource to the community. (Past image, courtesy YCHS.)

ne 1925 Newberg Berrian Festival (Rosarians included in picture) Memorial Park, Newberg.

Memorial Park is used year-round, not just during the Old Fashioned Festival. This city park sits in a neighborhood on the south side of town. It features a covered picnic area, bathrooms, a scout house, and a playground that is enjoyed by children through the year. (Past image, courtesy OHS.)

Hess Creek runs under Highway 99W and through Hoover Park. A bridge was initially built to take drivers over the creek. The layout of the park has changed, and there is no longer a bridge, but cars and pedestrians can still easily cross the creek on their way in and out of downtown. (Past image, courtesy GFU.)

PORTLAND BRIDGE FROM CITY PARK, NEWBERG, OREGON. W34.

Newberg has many city parks. One is named after a Newberg resident and the 31st president of the United States, Herbert Hoover. The park sits across the street from one of his childhood homes and has been updated multiple times. Today, it features a playground and nine-hole disc golf course. (Past image, courtesy OHS.)

The tall trees and quiet stream made Hoover Park a lovely place for a picnic. The banks of the stream are still a lovely place to visit today, but a nine-hole disc golf course now occupies the majority of the park, making it less suitable for a picnic and better for some casual competition with friends. (Past image, courtesy GFU.)

Pres. Herbert Hoover was born in West Branch, Iowa, but spent three years of his childhood living in Newberg with his aunt and uncle after his parents passed away. His home was heavily renovated by those who occupied it after he lived there, but It has since been restored to its original condition and is now open to the public as a museum. (Past image, courtesy GFU.)

Christmas On Willamette River at Newberg, Ore., 1924

The Willamette River has shaped not only Newberg, but the entire Willamette Valley and much of the state of Oregon. The river can be accessed in Newberg at Rogers Landing. It does not typically freeze like this picture from 1924, but the river can still be accessed here for a variety of water sports. (Past image, courtesy GFU.)

Travelers can follow the Willamette River downstream to Oregon City or upriver to Eugene. Although the river runs through Portland and connects to the Columbia, a lock system is needed to pass the Willamette Falls. The Willamette Falls Locks are awaiting repairs and will one day transport people along the entirety of the river again. Rogers Landing in Newberg offers a dock, boat ramp, and a great way to get out on the water, whether for transportation or recreation. (Past image, courtesy GFU.)

BIBLIOGRAPHY

Beebe, Ralph. *A Heritage to Honor, A Future to Fulfill.* Newberg, OR: The Barclay Press, 1991.

Doyle, Barbara. *Springbrook Oregon, Local: National: International.* Newberg, OR: Barbara Doyle, Nomadic Teacher Programs, 2017.

Fuller, Tom, and Christy Van Heukelem. *Newberg.* Charleston, SC: Arcadia Publishing, 2010.

Mapping Our History. libguides.georgefox.edu/c.php?g=1233138&p=9024466.

Newberg Public Library: Over 100 Years of Library Service. www.newbergoregon.gov/library/page/library-history-and-stories.

Zickefoose, Chuck. "History of the Red Electric Railroad in Newberg." Lecture for the Newberg Area Historical Society. www.youtube.com/watch?v=ODd4PqnSypo&t=574s.

DISCOVER THOUSANDS OF LOCAL HISTORY BOOKS
FEATURING MILLIONS OF VINTAGE IMAGES

Arcadia Publishing, the leading local history publisher in the United States, is committed to making history accessible and meaningful through publishing books that celebrate and preserve the heritage of America's people and places.

Find more books like this at
www.arcadiapublishing.com

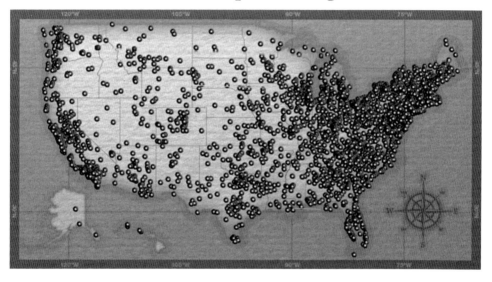

Search for your hometown history, your old stomping grounds, and even your favorite sports team.

Consistent with our mission to preserve history on a local level, this book was printed in South Carolina on American-made paper and manufactured entirely in the United States. Products carrying the accredited Forest Stewardship Council (FSC) label are printed on 100 percent FSC-certified paper.

MADE IN THE USA